The Everywhere God

Printed in the United States of America
First Printing, 2015
ISBN-13:978-1507533727

From Gigi
For Jessica, Ellie, Joey, Jordan, Rachel, Dain and my boy Ryan ~
So you would never forget how much he, and He, loves you.

From Marmee
For my children and grandchildren ~
May you always seek to know our God.

And for children everywhere.

On top of the list of the things you should know
Regardless the distance you may have to go,
Through winter's snow deep...

or summer's sun hot.
When you find yourself got in a difficult spot,
At that very minute, God's loving you in it.

Does time seem to stop?
Sure, often it does.

Are the wishes you wish
only wishes you wuz?

Do the dreams
and the schemes
and the
"I didn't means..."

Or the aches and mistakes
from awful bad breaks,

Make your day seem too long?
Well, God hasn't gone.

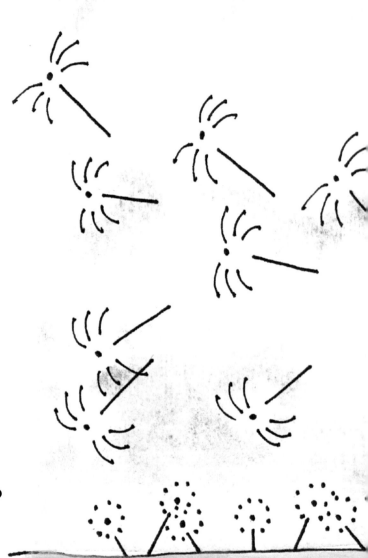

When you're in a pickle and don't have a nickel,
Got caught in a tree with a very mad bee,

Stuck tight in some hole with an unwelcome mole,
Or lost in a lair of a big hungry bear,
God won't let you down, He's always around.

If you make a wish of becoming a fish
And live in a lake with a long purple snake,

Turn into, of course, a small spotted horse...

And search through the day for some sugary hay.

Would God love you then?
Oh yes. Amen!

When things go all wrong and days seem too long,
Bad spills or strange ills lead to Doctor's pink pills,
If you're sent back to bed with a hot aching head...

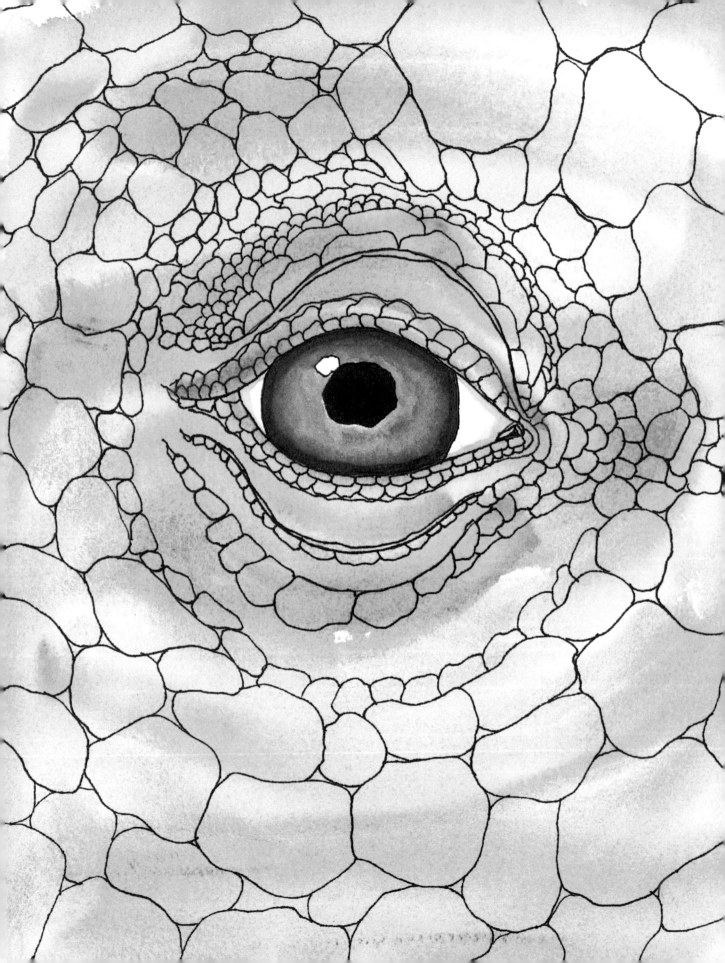

'Cause your temperature's high as a dinosaur's eye.
Can you then hear God say,
"Hey! You'll be O.K."?

You could casually stroll to the icy North Pole
Or crawl through the sand with a desert jazz band.
You could slip on a snail and land in some jail,
Or fly to the moon on a black-eyed racoon.

And God, it is true,
would be waiting on you.

On a mountain top high or the beach by the sea,
On the back of an eagle flying so free.
In a car, on a boat, by a fast train or plane...

Take a cab, ride a bike
or skate through the rain.
God sees with a smile and
He loves all the while.

If time-outs seem long, and you're all alone,
Or nobody called you today on the phone...

If Mommy is here and Dad's over there,
And often it seems there is no one to care.
God does and God loves,

'cause God's everywhere.

Your heart is God's home, forever and some.
His love never leaves you whatever will come.
When you need to hear Him, you can and you must,
He speaks through your parents
and friends you can trust.

The message comes quickly without any fuss,
The Everywhere God loves people like us.

Thank You!

This book would not be here had it not been for the support and contributions of our Kickstarter campaign funders. Each dollar you gave to fund this project means so much to us. We are SO grateful for your belief in this project. You will forever be a part of *The Everywhere God* story, telling people everywhere how much God loves them.

Thank you from the bottom of our hearts.

Angela and Aaron Anderson
Chris and Maggie Angelica
Becky Bales
Lee Bowers
Chan and Susan Nelson Brooks
Angela Caldwell
Jeff and Kathy Nelson Chambers
Laury Christensen
Steve and Jennifer Church
Linda and Joe Crawford
Michelle Schmitt Crawford
Daniel and Noel Goran
Barb Gritton
Jerry Hater
Sandie Hater-Koch
Jeanne Keith
Linda Kerdolff
Gwen Lambert
Maria Lester
Heidi and Mike Mack
Toni McClellan
Jill McGlone
Jenny Hall Medley
Christian and Chris Melton
Amy and Jason Meredith
Rankin Milburn
Karen Mobley

Betsy Murphey
Ann Nelson
Sam and Tootsie Nelson
Judi Cissell O'Bryan
Courtney Larkin Owens
Courtney and JP Park
Richard and Amy Polk
Cinda Pruitt
Sheryl Redmon
Susan Rose
Kelly and Evan Nelson Rowe
Ron and Vicky Rowe
Mark and Sandi Sansbury
Jennifer Henderson Simpson
Kenny and Tracey Smith
Elizabeth Spilman
Tom and Jami Springer
Scott and Dianne Tillman
Robert Tillman
Jim Trammell
Karen Turner
Sandy Veinot
Dan Vonderheide
Laura Wagner
Wendee Wyatt Walker
Michael and Amy Williams
Cindy Willison